ONE HUNDRED DROPS *of* WATER

RAÚL SÁNCHEZ MONREAL, JR.

principles of life-challenges & inspirations

MORGAN JAMES PUBLISHING • NEW YORK

ONE HUNDRED DROPS *of* WATER

Also available in Spanish / También disponible en Español

Paperback ISBN: 978-1-60037-013-7 (English version)

Paperback ISBN: 978-1-60037-230-8 (Spanish version)

Audio ISBN: 978-1-60037-014-4

Published by:

MORGAN · JAMES
THE ENTREPRENEURIAL PUBLISHER ™
www.morganjamespublishing.com

Morgan James Publishing, LLC
1225 Franklin Ave Ste 32
Garden City, NY 11530-1693
Toll Free 800-485-4943
www.MorganJamesPublishing.com

www.RaulSMonrealJr.com

Cover/Interior Design by:

Rachel Campbell
rcampbell77@cox.net

Habitat for Humanity®
Peninsula
Building Partner

DEDICATION *and* ACKNOWLEDGEMENT

This book is dedicated to Aurelia, my wife and my pillar, whose understanding and support has always been my driving force. To my son Raúl III, lovely wife Sally and our beautiful grandchild Sierra Nicole, daughter Clarissa and husband John Wiszezur, and son Orlando; All of who are my pure drops of water that have allowed me to be in spirit. My family was the core energy that moved me to publish this poetry book. The poetry book is also dedicated to my mother, Vickie Lowe, step-father Ernie Lowe, my sister, Hortencia and husband Guillermo Rodriguez, my mother-in-law, Guadalupe Amaya Romero and extended family. A special remembrance to my nephew Martin Rodriguez, his family, Grandmother Paz Barron and father-in-law, José Guillermo Amaya Romero.

I would like to thank Robin Thompson for acknowledging my poetry talent and for suggesting that I meet David Hancock from Morgan James Publishing LLC who immediately offered to assist me with the publishing in English and Spanish. To Chris Howard, Jim Howard,

Heather Kirk whose valuable assistance I could not have done without. To Chris Howard, Author Relations Manager, for guiding me on the first stages of the book.

PREFACE *One Hundred Drops of Water*

Poetry as an art form is a bridge to various inspirational emotions that touches a sensitive nerve that sends a signal to the heart. It is capable of assisting that special individual that purchase One Hundred Drops of Water in the same way a prism channels the light into the most vivid spectrum of colors from the rainbow causing a positive influence. The following body of work is evocative of the reaffirmation and optimistic spirit produced by examining one's life and learning experiences. Samuel Johnson was fond of saying that "vice is the consequence of narrow thoughts." As a rebuttal, this author's effort is the diametric opposite of those narrow thoughts. The sentiments related to the reader through this medium are varied and intense. The creative energy espoused herein touches upon spirituality, love, hope, friendship, meditation, divine experience, faith, romance and a positive cognitive process.

Considering the changing facets of each work will profoundly engage the recesses of the mind to yield dormant memories. Reasoned reflection upon humble origin, inauspicious beginning, encounter with self doubt or other sometimes debilitating human conditions is a valuable tool in maintaining the will and capacity to achieve objectives without succumbing to cynicism or bitterness. The messages proffered in this poetry seek connection to the desirable feelings of attainment, contentment and fulfillment which are the derivative results of maintaining balance in one's life.

The works are intended to be esthetically pleasing as well, with dynamic interplay between the most complex thoughts and words which may not always suffice to illustrate a point clearly. It is precisely why the poetry is so eloquent. The elements of flexibility, the universality of some experiences tailored to personal endeavor and empirical knowledge are a wonderful collaboration. The meaning of the work may change as clouds can change the look of the landscape. The truth contained therein with not.

Professor, Joseph A. Duarte

Professor, Rose S. Duarte

Author's Note

Since the birth of a dream to publish "One Hundred Drops of Water" where I could present personal inspirations to all who wish and wait for them was an incredible challenge that I couldn't resist see it to fruition. I am hoping to inspire and touch at least one fiber of each person who purchase "One Hundred Drops of Water" a collection of inspirations that come from the heart so they can enjoy with their own experiences combine with the sentiments of the special drops of water converted into poems that will bring out vivid moments of their own emotions. The diverse themes are living experiences and inspirations that were caused by my own lifelong learning. At the same time they are carefully selected by chosen words so to paint a vivid picture depicting a sublime and memorable time.

I also discovered that this is one way forum of presenting and allowing my poems for each and everyone who will be owners of "One Hundred Drops of Water" be able to experience the special inspiration within each poem. These hand picked poems is a testimony, mainly mine—with God giving directions to capture and then give the pure inspiration a voice (in spirit). It is also, so rare for me to open up to the public while creating an open door where you will be able to find out the intimacy relationship with the inspiration that I was born with. My poems are creations that coincide with the creation of songs that in my mind by having traditional rhyme follow by the melody that touches everyone's heart.

These poems are a personal anthology that I present to you as drops of water that unite without being able to determine the voice of that original inspiration but instead appear to be your own voice. They are also, inspirational words who are now converted into poems that narrate a specific glimpse of time and life.

These specially selected and collected poems are drops of water that when they come together they make universal identities without being able to tell them apart because they become as unique as you.

Raúl Sánchez Monreal, Jr.
POET

TABLE *of* CONTENTS

V

ONE HUNDRED DROPS *of* WATER

MY POEMS ARE CRYSTAL DROPS OF WATER FROM MY TEARS,
The joy of my heart like a delightful song to please your ears.

My inspirations chosen by my inner soul,
my failures and successes that I experienced as I grew old.

My poems are created with careful chosen words just for you,
producing a painting of lifelong experiences so vivid that is true.

My poems are sincere and they come to me frequently,
I put them on paper so you can inherit them instantly.

They are specially destined for people, who want them,
without a doubt with pleasure for those who await them.

I value everyone that likes to read them understanding its intent,
know that I wrote one hundred poems for you as a compliment.
So now, that my book of poetry is finish I dedicated to my readers,
in this beautiful treasure chest because you are my fearless leaders.

WE ARE DROPS *of* WATER

WHEN TWO DROPS OF WATER UNITE
no one can tell them apart.
This essence, so pure, is delight
fulfilling the thirst of the heart.

Every human being is a drop
so unique that is made out of love
when they unite it is hard to stop
creating a smooth transition from above.

Water is the source of life
because many drops came together
creating the nutrients to end all strife
the source of resources altogether.

Let's use this great example
where drops naturally become water,
all human being are ample
this is what we all want, my brother.

 My Poem

AN INSPIRATION CAME VIA MY MIND TO MY HEART.

The mind directed my hand with a pen and gave its part.

In the mind a plan was formulated and sent with a pen on hand,

I started and created a poem with good intent.

I watched the creation like a son of mine on its day view.

I caressed it and I gave it form, now I send it to you.

The satisfaction was so marvelous to see my work developed like a rose.

The pure significance that my poem aroused.

If you analyze it right,

You will understand my plight.

THE POET

WHEN A POET GETS IN SPIRIT AN INSPIRATION COMES,
the open mind captures the message and the poem becomes.

A poet opens all its senses without any limitation,
the conscious gets ready to send a signal with special emotion.

Many times a poet is critize for expressing its point of view,
but it doesn't matter because the poet is in control on what he construes.

What's to gain when you write poetry and share it with the reading fans?
The fact you did it and get a reaction when they buy the book
and get their thanks.

ASSION

AN INNER SPIRIT THAT MOVES YOU
a synergy of devotion in motion,
a strong deep feeling renewed
an intense desire is a passion.

A basic essential that thrives
a feeling within that is strong,
an intimate spirit that drives
I know that my passion belongs.

I am true to my inner feelings
for my thoughts I am thankful,
I adhere to my well-being
now my passion is so powerful.

When you find your alignment
your core passion will work for you,
when you are out of alignment
your core passion will not work, it's true.

VISIONARY

THE GIFT TO SEE BEYOND THE SEA
in spite of the many barriers on the way,
play the hand you have and see
you need to proceed using your sway.

Your mental vision seeks the truth
an ordinary person operates within his booth,
you can make abstract matter understood
yet a common person needs more proof.

Use all your senses to expand your vision
your mission then will come together,
separating yours from the competition
the steps you chose are right in order.

The magnetic force you exude
attracts the energy from others too.
Use it well and give it to those that care for others
helping humans being like your brothers.

CHARACTER

IT'S NOT ENOUGH TO BE,
we need to learn each day,
seek worth on what we see,
TRUSTWORTHINESS along the way.

Allow our minds to wonder
and ponder for a moment,
RESPECTING things encountered,
becoming life's proponents.

A decision must be made,
right or wrong is the exercise,
RESPONSIBILITY must not waver
because the choice is what makes us wise.

Keep in mind that we are not alone,
FAIRNESS is what counts in our society,
when we level the playing field for everyone,
it provides an individual with an opportunity.

When you want to make a difference,

and you feel it in your heart,

CARING makes it worthwhile

and you will know you did your part.

These are the ingredients for which we should opt

aligning the real CHARACTER in our daily lives.

Honoring those who respect these human traits and adopt

seeing these characteristics in a CITIZEN that thrives.

PRINCIPLES *for the* GOOD *of* HUMANITY

START THE DAY WITH A CLEAN SLATE

don't bring past problems to lament,

nor future desires to contemplate

let us use today, our present.

Next in line we must create value for others

expect nothing in return,

this nurtures the spirit much further

allowing the source to prolong.

Now, you build relationships

empowering the team to succeed,

moving in the same direction

reaching the goal you conceived.

The goal is to make a difference

making this world better to live in

our next generation divergence.

What difference did we leave?

$\mathscr{I}$ KNOW I CAN So I *don't* FEAR

TODAY'S THE DAY THAT I CAN REACH

my wants and wishes will come true.

I'm blessed to do so without fear.

My dreams are ever so near and clear.

I will not dwell on yesterday,

nor wait until tomorrow.

I have my full day, today,

no extra time to borrow.

So here is my gift, I leave with you,

just a thought to ponder.

Everybody fears fear.

even fear fears itself;

So confront your fear,

and fear will disappear

as success will eventually appear.

So now you understand

that I know I can...

so I don't fear.

FRIEND RAISING

THE AMAZING ART OF GIVING,
allowing all to know,
understanding and believing
the funding tends to flow.

Don't try to get the money first
if you don't know the cause,
because the cause will win you
and you will earn the applause.

A human being tends to give.
This is its instinct from within.
it is the cause that we believe
so our children grow and win.

This is better known to us:
friend raising for a cause.
The focus is all of us
the funding is the plus.

DREAM all YOU CAN BE

WITHIN ME, I SENSE AN INSPIRATION.

A message is sent to my mind.

A dream is captured in motion.

The creative message defined.

The clarity of the unpublished dream,

sends words to the graphic mind

receiving a picture via a beam.

Creating a painting so vivid is divine.

The painting now turns to poetry.

Uniting those special parts

to me is known as pure creativity,

uplifting our hearts.

Now, I have a Dream.

Its essence is all it can be.

Now, I put it to practice:

A message so unique, I let it be.

REACH *for the* STARS

I KNOW WE CAN, SO WE DON'T FEAR,

the words "We can't" have disappeared

with mind and spirit we persevere

because the words "We Can" are here.

You see my friends this says it all,

that how we feel has been revealed.

Let's take a stand and understand

that yes, "We Can," achieve it all.

Reach for the stars,

while our dreams are so near.

They'll never be far,

if we see past our fear.

Reach and be touched,

we'll like how we feel.

But don't say too much,

act now and be fulfilled.

We all feel good,

when we face the truth.

And trace the way

to where we stood.

When we find the light

shining bright

the time is right

and your angels are in sight.

Reach and be touched

and see that you're there

and just be aware

that success is everywhere

we are!

PROCRASTINATION

WHEN YOU DECIDE TO STAY IDLE
and the world is on the move
the best of life will pass you
then you feel the blues.

You are a special person
with a gift for you to use
use your faith and move on
procrastination will be gone.

Your life is full of tools
and also gifts of mind
don't waste them like fools
don't let them stay behind.

Procrastination is a problem
for those who, idle, stay
on the move is the solution
and gratification on the way.

We Must Act

To be the best you must act,
don't delay the drive within.
Be on the move and don't react
believe in yourself and win.

When you get a feeling to move
and you begin to doubt.
Allow your instinct to prove
that special feeling you caught.

Your decision produces action
when you see beyond the now.
It's the reality that brings satisfaction
and the outcome will make you proud.

The name of the game is you
the key to success is your action.
Give your attention to detail in full
and you will realize your creation.

IMPOSSIBLE

ONE WAY TO AVOID ANY CHALLENGE
is to use the word impossible.
It's an easy way not to face a change
and later realize it was plausible.

Impossible is a word that is thrown around
by those who view their world small by their nature,
satisfied in their routine, disregarding fertile ground
but then they question or blame others for their failure.

Impossible is not a reality. It is merely an excuse.
Fear factor controls the mind, thinking you are immune.
Wonder why you are idle or why you feel abused?
You created false expectations and your energy was consumed.

So impossible is an opinion and a state of mind.
you either like the way it feels or prefer to stay behind.
When the word impossible is used you also feel confined
change impossible to possible and take away the blinds.

To Fail

IF YOU ARE AFRAID TO FAIL

when you need to act

leaving behind no trail

you will be forced to react.

This is no way to start the day

don't be a coward.

Because you become prey

stopping you from moving forward.

A solution to this dilemma

is to act without fear of failing.

You can always try a new plan

moving forward will prevail.

So to fail is better than to remain still.

Gaining your edge reaching your goal,

allowing your being to have a free will

you can regain your total control.

INNOVATOR

A THINKER ALLOWS HIS MIND TO CREATE,

waves passing by then they are captured,

replace them with words to procreate,

the image appears like pure nature.

An innovator is creative,

allowing inspiration to come alive,

adding meaning and revive,

a vivid picture that survives.

An inventive mind,

creates energy that blends,

allowing beauty to combine,

allowing an explosion that amends.

We know this is known as an innovator,

because from thin air beauty appears,

creation evolves uniting its color,

innovation allows anyone to be a creator.

Brain power used and focused

opportunities are very potent

levels of maturity have a cause

resources acquired and feel content.

apparent now and here.

SYNERGY

SYNERGY EMITTED AND COMMITTED
captured process to its fullest
value each person fitted
outcomes that linger with results.

Brain power used and focused
opportunities are very potent
levels of maturity have a cause
resources acquired and feel content.

Don't try to be somebody you are not
be yourself, you are unique and people feel it
Your expression is the nourishment people talk about
the highest form of synergetic relationship.

So when you're feeling nourished as one
and you begin to notice the urge to express
Effective synergies are synergies that honor everyone
they will feel supported in organically evolving your caress.

EMPOWERMENT

EMPOWERMENT IS A PROCESS THAT IS SHARED,
allowing skills, abilities and creativity to nourish.
While accepting ownership and accountability to dare
allowing control and a decision that will flourish.

Empowerment is an essential process
so that any human being can contribute in his or her own way
growth and his potential as he faces success
making a difference for someone else every day.

Empowerment is used for different causes.
At times it is use to unify the masses
and sometimes to address the messes,
that is unjust to certain human classes.

Empowerment is a powerful process
to better the world peace and enhance the harmony
and to be able to use the world resources
to bring the best from you and me.

An Opinion

DON'T CRITIZE MY WORDS
until you have a chance to analyze them.
Listen to my advice because if you don't,
our objectives will be apart pointing fingers and blame.

Let's leave our destructive pride aside,
this will only cause us to fight.
instead let's complete the quest.
It is so beautiful, when unity exists.

You work better if it is allow
for a good friendship and prosperity.
Tell me something, my friend and I will follow
I will listen intently and you will know, it's worth the unity.

HANGE

ACCEPT OURSELVES AS WE ARE,
change desires that we are not
look inside us not out far,
don't let it be a hidden plot.

Accept what we cannot change,
don't try to emulate another person.
Learn about you, don't be a stranger to yourself,
remember we are each a special person.

Accept what we can change,
face the truth don't circumvent.
We deserve a second chance,
even though peer pressure prevents.

If we change, accept responsibility
make adjustments and move precisely,
that change depends on your sincerity
and the tranquility you feel inwardly.

If change never really happens to us
it's because when it happens, it's rejected,
not just by us but those around us
embracing the change will protect us.

In fact, the change itself needs to be accepted
but changes that come along with the change:
one thing leads to other, they are connected.
the paradigm needs to shift to be exchanged.

EDUCATION

WHAT IS AN EDUCATION?

Is it an interruption?

I would say that's our salvation.

Allow me to explain, what I meant.

It is evident that our problems destroy us.

It is that we do not take into account, education.

That's the reason that we cause harm to each other,

I believe that education can bring a positive change.

The contrary, it can regain consequences

and this is not a goal we want to gain.

Let's provide our children with the education they deserve

so they don't have to suffer a bad situation.

Preoccupation is a good word to use, to be enriched.

If you aren't preoccupied about your family,

no one else is going to be.

Should Education Be *this* Way

⌒

I WAS BORN POOR YET EDUCATION LIES DEEP WITHIN ME
The teaching methods and techniques that were used in our school
Were also used in the time my grandparents attended in
their neighborhood.
Unfortunately, a portion of my people continues to work in the fields.
And I don't know why, but maybe they were not on the honor list
that yields.
I continue to analyze this, as the reason not to fail.
I assure you that my willingness to learn is strong yet lack of
attention prevails.
Allow me a little of your time and let me explain a living creature.
The way education is presented by certain dictators claiming to
be teachers.
I am telling you because I have experienced and felt this frustration.
I don't understand why in this century they continue to teach without
any consideration
I have heard that those who teach us first are our parents.
But certain teachers confuse us and they tell us, don't even think of
speaking to lament.

Because what you know and bring to the class has no value

What I teach you is all correct and understand it or I will paddle you

It is so difficult to want and feel helpless

To help my teachers so they can help me understand

My teachers tell me to always tell the truth

But it is sad that they know that what they are teaching us

For our future lives many times has no value

So to all of you, please let me know, even though I barely know you

How am I going to let them know, that I am intelligent, want to

better myself

want to contribute to our society, but the times are tough for me.

Like Cesar Chavez said, "Si Se Puede" "Yes, It Can Be Done,"

Like I said, "Si Se Debe," "It Is Right,"

Like President Fox said, 'Si Se Pudo," "Yes, Now It Is Done."

THE HISPANIC
STUDENT

~

LISTEN MY FRIEND, WHY DO YOU CRITIZE MY SPOKEN ENGLISH?

If you review the real circumstances as they really are,

everything you say is the opposite.

What you want is to make my life miserable,

so that I get disillusioned and don't reach my desired objective.

You are constantly reminding me of my accent,

but the truth of the matter is your jealousy that I speak my language

and your language; without a doubt this troubles you in the present.

I speak my language with honor,

also your language and I don't make a big fuss.

But it is time to set the story straight so that you know

all the things that you ignore,

and watch yourself on the mirror.

That way you will be able to understand yourself.

The persons who lower others because they destroy true talent,

they are like snakes which one day they will view themselves the same way.

I don't know why it is necessary to give nasty details,

but sometimes it is needed so that you stop and keep your mouth shut

don't corrupt.

Look, I already analyze the way you think,

and I am not going to allow you to hurt my people.

because I will assure you that I will not stand still silent.

Notice that I am not an ignorant, nor an uncivilized animal.

I am going to show you that I am an educated person.

This may turn into strong forceful dialogue,

If this is the way you operate then we have made progress

because you will analyze everything you say, write and study.

A GREAT TEACHER: Rose Duarte

IN AN ATTEMPT TO THANK A GREAT TEACHER
I am going to attempt to describe her qualities.
she has broad knowledge of subject matter
but her passion shows clearly her abilities.

A love of learning transmitted to her students
curriculum and standards use to open minds
while maintaining a caring attitude that compliments
with a desire that make a difference to mankind.

Knowledge of discipline and to keep up to date
with classroom management techniques
challenging daily students potential and their fate
having faith is just as important with her work she seeks.

As you can see the description of a great teacher in this poem
hope this portrays that special person in my life
Rose Duarte is that great teacher I am talking about
I am who I am because this great teacher ended my strife.

LEARNING *with* a PURPOSE

LEARNING IS AN INSTINCT,

with a purpose in the mind.

Learning how to get it,

leaving ignorance behind.

We all have a need to learn

from knowledge that surrounds us.

We just need to decide

to take advantage, making progress.

Learning is so natural.

Mind nutrients you don't force,

allowing wisdom to flourish

changing our life's future course.

Learning is not taught,

it needs to be desired,

knowing where to find it,

then use what's acquired.

OPE

No person can be without it.

if you have it you are blessed,

without it you are mess,

adding to your life stress.

How do you make sure?

If all of us can have it,

faith is the key to ensure it

then you act on it.

A belief that is alive,

expectation just waiting

to be use in any moment

by the person that is daring.

An aspiration worth seeking

on a belief that is there

I made it my promise

that's why I am aware.

My hope is my belief

I know what's require,

the more I prolong

the more value acquired.

Our Challenge

Life is a challenge, I think we all know.

Some face reality, some face the unknown.

Yet at the end we learn to survive

by changing the ways we live our lives.

When times are tough, we blame the world.

When times are good, we forget the world.

Money is the factor that creates the greed.

Stress enters our body and we begin to bleed.

Body toxins are many, reasons for losing our health

Not even wealth gets rid of the hell

We tune our bodies out disregarding reality

When we enter the quicksand we lack vitality.

No wonder why the world can turn on all of us.

When in fact we should say, the problem I own.

Blaming does very little for our soul.

The truth is the answer, so let's make it our goal.

$\mathcal{I}$ Know *we* Can

I KNOW WE CAN, SO WE DON'T FEAR

The words "<u>We can't</u>" have disappeared

our mind and spirit perseveres,

because the words "We Can" are here.

So you see my friends, this says it all

that how we feel has been revealed.

So let's take a stand and understand.

So reach for the stars

while our dreams are so near.

They'll never be far,

if we see past our fear.

So reach and be touched

we'll like how we feel

but don't say too much,

just act now and be fulfilled.

We all feel good,

when we face the truth

and trace the way

to where we stood.

When we find the light,

shining so bright,

the time is right,

and the angels are always in sight.

So reach for the stars

while our dreams are so near.

They'll never be far

if we see past our fear.

Reach and be touched

and see that you're there

and just be aware

that success is everywhere

we are!

Don't be In the Way

EVERY HUMAN BEING ON EARTH

was born with survival skills.

The test of life came at birth

making the road full of thrills.

As we grow we face struggles.

Some face them head on,

some wear their goggles,

while others move on.

Individuals who are insecure

make it difficult for others,

while others go around the curves

staying focused, ignoring all the clutters.

If you choose to ignore it and stay

don't hold back those who move on,

stay focused. Don't be in the way

reach for your dream and run.

My Illusions

ILLUSIONS WE ALL HAVE
realizing them is what we dare,
stresses that we embark
see our dreams reach that mark.

Most of the time we neglect
our beloved it human beings,
'because we involve on our illusions
goals that we want to achieve.

The illusions are so ambitious
that makes us start right away,
the visions that we want achieve
the songs I want to lay a way.

They are the essence of my thoughts
with all of you, I want to reach
so that I can give them to you
all my songs that I will sing.

Now, I dedicate this song

to my family with my emotions,

don't think that I don't love you

I prefer all of you, you're my devotion.

I respect them 'cause of their patience

their intelligence gives me my conscious,

there is no doubt of my love for them

just having them is a great honor.

JEALOUSY TALKS *to* ALL *of* US

I SEE WHAT IS HAPPENING AMONG US AND I AM SADDENED

I see those who make it and forget about their people angering me.

I see that among us there is no respect,

I see an ignorance that runs along the way.

I see that there are no models for those who we want to be educated.

I see some wanting to do it but we turn our face so that we are

not disturb.

I see that some people want to be empowered,

I see the line destroy so that they won't be bothered.

I see that we fight among ourselves because we are manipulated.

I see that we don't love each other this is because we are not united.

I see we lack the guts. That's the reason we lose our culture,

I see that is better to die fighting for our rights that to live

without direction

I see that we neglect our history.

I see people selecting defeat for not wanting to put the time in,

to be a successful person.

I see the low satisfaction of my people and this hurts all of us.

I see betrayals that make us lose focus

I see we use rhetoric a lot.

I see that we should use it in good practice as advice in a conversation.

I see our time disappearing.

I see what is happening for neglecting to pay attention to the science/

nature to get to know them.

I see that envy and jealousy are presents in this poem

I see that we now understand it and we need to destroy this

jealousy contract

I see that jealousy presents us with a good lesson

I see that we evaluate ourselves and we are will break this contract

and collaborate.

It's More *than* Just Getting Here

I HAVE LEARNED THAT NOT EVERYTHING IS ABOUT WINNING,

at times it is better to just get there,

and to trace the road.

I have valued the inquietude

because it has its virtue.

and my destined is in my control,

because this way, triumph tastes better,

without having to leave behind,

My principles.

It is so beautiful to harvest,

the good friendship created

and to tell you that you are valued,

like José Alfredo said in his song.

It fills us with emotion,

that is not about getting there first.

What is valued is to get there

and to make a better moment

in this world of truth.

When Enough is Enough

THE BIGGEST EXCUSE IS THAT WE DON'T HAVE *ENOUGH*
we have great ideas yet procrastinate.
Then fear takes a special place in the race
no action is taken but we are quick to react.

More of not ENOUGH surfaced
creating a fuss and no action.
I need more money is the claim
but the emotions lack the motion.

When is ENOUGH, not ENOUGH?
When we have ideas but no guts.
Even if the idea fails you get tough
and you gain the experience on this plot.

The way to survive in this vicious cycle:
move forward on your having ENOUGH.
Then follow you instincts; don't create obstacles
because your actions will smooth all the rough spots.

I Fell *in* Love *with* You

I FELL IN LOVE WITH YOU, WITH YOU,

I don't why with you,

nor why I chose you.

but it's the way it feels.

Is good and its true

that's the reason why, I love you.

I fell in love with you, with you,

I don't why with you,

nor why I chose you.

but it's the way it feels.

Is good and its true

that's the reason why, I love you

I will give you all my love,

and I will also offer my heart,

and you will feel the way I feel

you will recognize, my love.

69

$\mathscr{F}$RIENDSHIP *is* POSSIBLE

YOUR PASSIONATE LOOK
your messages well received
they were noted and captured
and they are deep within me .

You kept your decision in silence
to give to me a tiny space
it is so beautiful and exclusive
I thank you, I am blessed.

When I felt her friendly arms
I felt that inner peace that provides me
realizing my dreams and ignoring failures
with the friendship that you gave me.

With the magic of your eyes
with that look that is so cordial
and those beautiful red lips
a desired so special and jovial.

The friendship of this man,

to you and for your loyalty

you are now accustomed

from our years and our nobility.

We never set any conditions

simply committing ourselves

adding our God-given gifts

with all the faith and prays.

MOTHER, YOUR *special* DAY

LET'S CELEBRATE, MOTHER, YOUR SPECIAL DAY.

As an honor, we dedicate your song in a special way

You that gave me much happiness, life and adoration.

The heaven fills the air with inspiration.

Falling stars with special lights exemplify your novelty.

Mother, you are the highness

because we know you.

With flowers from my garden I give you fragrance.

My gratitude for all the tired nights you sacrificed

close to my crib, always giving me your special touch.

For your unconditional persistence,

Mother, immaculate lady,

you deserve a merit so divine,

a sacred place in heaven.

On this special day mother, you are glorified.

In your window diverse birds with their colorful feathers

sing to you, "Happy Birthday," Mother.

In unison with nature they made your day better.

The morning delighted with birds and that special sound,

making this poem a unique gift for you,

With words representing you and all your family

embracing you, like the waves at the sea,

celebrating you together with your children, Mother,

this is why we honor this special day to you.

 My Family

My beloved it wife, my lovely sons and daughter,

all I have and what I do is because they support me.

My work requires much time and preparation,

because my family understands that all the sacrifice.

was worth it so they all could have a good education.

I am fortunate man because their support allows me to be educated.

I ask God to protect them from harm

otherwise all I have accomplished will be in vane.

I have an educated wife that is beautiful and understanding

that gets along with me and we have an active grand time.

All our children are product of this relationship that accepted our role

as parents.

They are the most valuable jewels we have, reason that maintain

us together,

I pray that our patience continues its beautiful course forever,

because of our hard work will have been blessed,

and our children all of them will someday be educated

contributing to our society and serving as role models.

OUR SPECIAL
GRANDCHILD: *Sierra Nicole*

ON A SPECIAL DAY OF SEPTEMBER, OUR GRANDCHILD WAS BORN
and the nine months of waiting finally ended.
A gorgeous Grandchild announced with a cry, I'm home,
her parents and grandparents lifted her with pride.

The entire place knew who Sierra Nicole was.
For the first time she heard the miraculous applause.
She started to look and smile to her parents and us
Sierra felt her grand welcome and liked what she caused.

Sierra and Parents went from the hospital to their beautiful home
When the parents open the door Romeo, the dog said, Hi! with a bark.
Sierra Nicole felt the special energy, now in her Throne
Enjoying the home toy environment like it was a special park.

Now, Sierra Nicole is one year old, she walks, and runs all over
experiencing the mysteries of life; knowing she belongs.
At grandparent's home she meets new friends and does tricks
giving hugs and kisses, so now her love is very strong.

We thank God and the angels, who no doubt did their part

sending Sierra Nicole, an angel so special and blessed.

We pray each day, that we will never be apart

because she is our joy and to the Lord, we will always praise.

Yes You Can

A Poem dedicated to César E. Chávez

Every body responds out loud – Yes You Can!

They used to say that farm workers did not have rights like the rest of us
César E. Chávez arrived and boycotted the grapes, changing theories
and other things
Yes, You Can!

They used to say that no one will reach the moon
Now is history, we got there and came back like the foam.
Yes, You Can!

They used to say that we will never see a Hispanic as a state governor
Several have made it, executing the laws with intelligence.
Yes, You Can!

They used to say that we will never see programs that help minorities
This situation was changed because it was a bad theory.
Yes, You Can!

They used to say that we will always be at the bottom

If we decide to change all negative forces we will do it we just need

to believe.

Yes, You Can!

Let us take advantage of the education that is there for those who

wanted

This will bring a positive change for our people and each one of you

deserves it.

Yes, You Can!

I am glad that you understand what I am trying to tell you

That we will do our part and that way we can teach them.

Yes, You Can!

It appears that we decided to be just to each other and this does not hurt

On the contrary, my friends, Let's climb higher and go ahead because

Yes, You Can! Yes, You Can! Yes, You Can!

WHAT I LEARNED has VALUE

I HAVE CAUSED A WOUND
and it won't heal,
I left my family at the river
trying to cross for real
believing that on the other side
I would leave behind being poor.

In my birth land I suffered
seeing my sons cry
because they asked for food
but I couldn't give them what they wanted
they went to sleep being hungry
and weak as they went to work.

I left my beloved birthplace
my parents and my friends
exchanged them for few coins
and abuses from some bandits
because they would not allow me
to gain a salary because they will steal it.

What's the purpose of this torment

if I am not asking for credit?

Just some honest work to earn

without taking work from anyone

but they continue to ridicule me

when I am doing my job.

After trying to reason

now that I feel so lonely

you will see hatred in my eyes

because of others that were lazy

and left a lot destruction

for being dishonest and traitors.

I hope I have learned the lesson

That the dollar is not everything in our lives

Now I am very frustrated

and on this side feeling I am in a cage.

THE EARTH is CRYING

IF YOU CAN ASPHYXIATE ME, YOU WOULD DO IT,

If you need to confront me, you will be quiet,

at the end, you lose.

You have change our fertile ground for your convenience,

You have harm my lungs for your imprudence,

at the end, you lose.

Enough!...enough!

Look at my face, I am crying

Enough!...enough!

your cruelty is killing me.

In the jungle the noises are calling you,

in the music of the seas there is a message,

at the end, you lose.

You have opened a wound, with your greediness,

starting the end of the rest of your days,

at the end, you lose.

Enough!...enough!

Look at my face, I am crying

Enough!...enough!

your cruelty is killing me.

The earth needs our help,

let's plant stars

instead mutilating its wonders.

HEARTS of MEN AFFECT

IF YOU WANT TO CHANGE YOUR LIFE,
you can lift yourself by your thoughts,
then you must dream,
because high achievement brings many rewards.

Fame comes when we act on what we know,
while other successes come from on what they do
yet success comes because of who they are now
and through this poem, hope and luck turn to you.

Find opportunities that lie in the midst of difficulty,
while every problem has hidden in it an opportunity.
Make the situation reveal to you its prosperity
Men are mentors and mentoring means valuing creativity.

Lifetime, relationships teach us lifetime lessons,
those things you must build upon for a sound foundation.
Our job is to accept the lessons and value others,
It is said that love is blind but friendship a creation of two.

DIFFICULT

IT WILL BE DIFFICULT TO ACCEPT THE TIME YOU WENT AWAY

I won't be able, to get use to this loneliness.

I got used to the love that you once gave

today, I lost your friendship

I lie, if I tell you that I don't care.

Is been a year that I am trying to come back to you.

You will see the goodness of our life

finding that love of yesterday

I know that you feel like I do.

I predict that our lives will be reborn

my darling, check and see how I hurting too.

that my intent is to recapture our love

it is time for that longed-for moment

that will root this beautiful love.

Don't let yourself be taken by the opposition

that our love has true value not a competition.

Now, I understand that promise we made

with a kiss that sealed that pleasure

I admit, that yesterday I failed you.

But now, I promise all my love

I know you feel like I do

and I feel our lives will start all over

you are my beloved, check it out now

that my intent is to love you forever.

ONEY

THEY SAY THAT WITH MONEY I CAN DO ANYTHING
To a certain extent this might be true,
Even though health comes first
and later love from a noble heart.

A lot of us get confused by money,
believing that we can buy health and love.
Stumbling during our lives throughout the world
crying about our dissolutions without control.

Money that is earned lasts longer.
It lends to our lives so we have fun.
Control it without throwing it toward foolish ventures.
and millionaire you will feel , you'll see.

If you have faith and have health, you are rich.
you will enjoy your life in its totality,
and balancing the money that we earned
will give us even more happiness.

LARISSA

CLARISSA,

you are so beautiful,

with your cherry lips inviting

and so tempting my taste.

Clarissa,

you are my great surprise

while appearing so delicate

Creating such sensation!.

You are,

the woman I wished for,

the one for whom I felt such love

lost my sense to passion.

Tell me

that you love me.

I like the way it feels,

My feelings soar.

Clarissa,

you are my princess.

that takes away my sadness

give me your love.

Clarissa,

my most valuable gift

always give me your frankness

I love you so fervently.

You are,

the human being that I wished for,

the one I felt in love with

lost my sense to passion.

Tell me,

that you love me

I like the way it feels

My feelings soar.

$\mathscr{I}$ Am Yours

It is so nice to reach the zenith
with my fans on my side;
this allows me to sing.
In this respect they abide.

I want them to know
that I am yours
and my singing
is just for you.

You gave me friendship,
my faithful fans,
and immense loyalty
you made it happen.

I owe them everything
that I have earned
and with their applause
I can sustain.

With my language

I create emotions

that you all take

to every corner.

The day that my singing voice leaved me

and no longer plays in your hearts

that's the day I will die

with all my songs.

.

I give you thanks

with all my songs,

giving you homage

for your faithful attention.

I sing to my fans

who still love me,

that's why I tell you

that I am yours.

I give thanks

Will all my songs.

I pay you homage

For your attention.

Our Rhythm
is the Cumbia

❧

IN A TOWN CLOSE TO HERE
they like to listen to music,
when they play a Cumbia
everybody starts to dance.

The curious thing about the town
is that everybody knows each other
they dance Cumbia with anybody
even if past midnight.

They are all fanatics
dancing the Cumbianera
They are all fanatics
with music in the Riviera

They are all fanatics
creating a lot of dust,
They are all fanatics
making an immense circle.

In the dancing floor all knows each other

In particular singular pair

that they dance very different

with their original step.

Don Raúl and Doña Aurelia

is the dancing pair indicated

when they dance Cumbianera

they are always the best.

ϑONORA *and* IT'S CUMBIA

THE CUMBIA OF SONORA HAS A LOT OF FLAVOR

When you listen to the Cumbia all the girls move their waist

And then those girls are so contagious causing us to go crazy

Then we all lose it and they trap us with their beauty.

The Cumbia is for dancing

The Cumbia is for listening

You like it and you listen

with beautiful girls.

In Sonora they dance

the Cumbia has flavor

and even the Divas

like to show their bellies.

The Cumbia of Sonora is a rhythm so precious

They rich people dance and even the famous

It doesn't discriminate the Cumbia of Sonora

That's the reason in the dances this rhythm is contagious.

The Cumbia is my rhythm

A fabulous rhythm

The poor enjoys it

And even the rich.

Everybody likes it over there in Sonora

And anybody will dance it

When you listen it traps you

And sooths our ears.

The Cumbia of Sonora plays at any time

The Cumbia is happy and every likes it

It contagious happiness and it makes you smile

The Cumbia of Sonora is the rhythm I enjoy every day.

CUMBIA SAHUARIPENSE

THE OPATAS LEFT US
a piece of land, my brothers
and they offer us
their marvelous feeling.

Founders, they became
of Sahuaripa Sonora.
Their traditions captivated us
the one who visits, adores it.

Why, why you may say?
Why so many beautiful ladies?
Why, why you may say?
Because is in the blood of the mothers.

Why, why you may say?
Why do we make easy friends?
Why, why you may say?
They even come from Nogales.

Sahuaripa gets decorated

with its regional festivities

and all the neighbors come

with its musical groupies.

All fads are seen in the dance floor

with the corridos and cumbias

the men make their own list

venture loves seem very clear.

In Sonora you enjoy

the regional festivities,

her gentle beautiful people

from Sahuaripa to Nogales.

With its delicious food

its music and tequilas

with Bacanora we toast,

yell with family and friends.

CUMBIANDO

OH, OH, OH,
Oh, Oh, Oh, dance it for me

I am Cumbia, Cumbiando
dancing, singing and yelling
I am Cumbia, Cumbiando
enjoying this natural rhythm.

I am Cumbia, Cumbiando
bending your body to the dance
I am Cumbia, Cumbiando
it looks like I am in command.

I invite you to dance Cumbia
with your partner and natural rhythm.
I invite you to dance Cumbia
because when dance you feel the freedom.

Cumbia, Cumbia, Cumbiando
with your partner and natural rhythm

103

Cumbia, Cumbia, Cumbiando

creating an ambiance full of fun.

CONQUEST *in* MIAMI

WHILE ON VACATION
in Miami I began to stare.
At a beautiful Cuban lady
on the sea, where I decided to dare.

Suddenly, I spoke to her
and I told her a few beautiful things,
She responded with some care
thanks for the nice things you said.

Tell me, tell me, that you will stay,
tell me, tell me, that you will go my way,
give me, give me, just one reason,
give me, give me, my heart feels your passion.

I invited her for a short walk,
so that we can start knowing each other.
Suddenly, I kiss her as we stopped,
I enjoyed her love, you are now my lover.

Oh, my darling,

her exquisite lips pronounce to me.

Kiss me again, like I am doing,

my skin got a little chills in disbelieve.

Tell me, tell me, that you will kiss me,

tell me, tell me, that you will love me,

give me, give me, all your love,

give me, give me, that nice surprise.

Tell me, tell me, that you will stay,

tell me, tell me, that you will go my way,

give me, give me, just one reason,

give me, give me, my heart feels your passion.

$\mathcal{A}$DJUST *to the* RHYTHM

EVERYBODY GET OUT AND DANCE
adjust to the Rhythm,
the dance has unique movements
and you will feel its freedom.

Take a step to the front
your partner takes a step back,
take her from the waist
and make sure you stay on track.

Move her to the sides
give yourselves a turn,
finishing face to face
and a tight squeezes in return.

Give yourselves a nice smile
and let's start once again,
that the ambiance is happy
and you will know you gain.

 NOEMY

I INVITE YOU TO DANCE NOEMY.
together we will both celebrate,
I promised you
an ambiance of happiness.

With Noemi I will dance
rhythms from different regions.
I even sang her a song,
songs of different grand styles with visions.

We will dance a Quebradita.
We will dance a Rancherita.
We will dance a Cumbiadita,
and one or two Norteñitas.

We will dance a Rumba.
We will dance a Salsa.
We will dance a Mambito,
and one more cheek to cheek.

We will dance a Quebradita.

We will dance a Rancherita.

We will dance a Cumbia,

and one or two Norteñitas.

We will dance a Rumba.

We will dance a Salsa.

We will dance a Mambito,

and one more cheek to cheek.

$\mathcal{L}$OST SHADOW

I AM

the lost shadow

a wounded soul

in your heart.

I am

a forgotten object

a picture trace

that caused an emotion.

That hurts

loving without being loved

allowing to be forgotten

without any merit.

The life

is always repeated

and trying to get even

a false love.

If despise

harvest the shadow

sometimes it surprises

our own being.

Don't forget

your turn is now

a deep hit

so we understand.

And now

your soul cries

your time has come

and you don't need to wait.

MERRY CHRISTMAS
and a NEW
DIVINE NEW YEAR

~

THE MONTH OF DECEMBER STARTED

and a peaceful wind embraces us,

Reminding us of the Love that God gave us.

The earth in places is cover with white pure snow.

In this world all human beings give themselves presents with pleasure

The moment announces the birth of a saint, a holy creature.

The North Star shines and illuminates all of us,

an indication that God shows us the good road to take.

Dresses the night with diamonds using the stars above

with the colors that warm us like the red coals.

Let's give thanks, so our families enjoy good health

and that food may always be plentiful on the tables of each home.

You have liberated us from the work that turns to slavery

I am asking God to grant more than one wish.

That HE continues to protect us and to educate us,

so that we can understand what we yearn for,

Lord protect your poor children from injustices of the world.

This way Christmas will fill everyone with happiness every infinite second.

As human beings we should love each other

Merry Christmas and A Divine new Year to all.

PLEASE

PLEASE, DECIDE
it is necessary to know,
if you accepted my love
or you decided to let it go.

Please, get close to me
it is you I adore
I want to love you
I cannot wait anymore.

You are the reason I exist
I won't deny it any longer,
every day grows even more
my love for you grows stronger.

You see our love is now reality
I am drowning for you, this is true,
you have given me kindness
with the love I just found in you.

You are the reason of I exist

I won't deny it any longer,

every day grows even more

my love for you grows stronger.

You see our love is now reality

I am drowning for you, this is true,

you have given me kindness

with the love I just found in you.

I Feel *so* Lonely

I feel so lonely
I lost my love
and with this wine
I feel just fine.

My friend, please tell me
what I have done
my soul is crying.
This is no time for fun.

I gave of me
everything she wanted.
She didn't respond
from her soul.
Without her
I'm just a hopeless fool.

Remember this.
Don't be so stubborn,
She won't comeback.

she found a new lover,

so leave the drinking

and get back to your life.

Now I don't drink,

it doesn't matter.

You see my friends

everything is shattered.

This constant habit

it baffles the mind.

I lost my gal,

but I still got my wine.

I lost my gal,

but I still got my wine

CLOSE to US is the UNITY

~

CLOSE TO US IS OUR UNION,
remembering that lovely night
of that friendship we shared
on a sea so serene.

The moon embraced each of us
as we both murmured lovingly
listen to her lovely voice
under beautiful shining stars.

Christmas night o Christmas night
I'm desperate when I want to see her
to revive that love of mine
to savor for a short time.

Christmas night o Christmas night
as I remember that Christmas night,
I want to be together like yesterday
under the full moon's brilliant face.

119

We are together once again,

we are not going to split again,

because we need each other

and the warmth we create together.

I Went *to* the UNITED STATES

I LEFT FOR THE UNITED STATES

looking for a good job.

Over there my friends

are really having fun.

Don't let it deceive you.

What they say is not true.

Don't think that everything is fun

Sometimes everything feels deserted.

Life is not how they view it

It is hard and our souls grow tired.

The bosses promise many things

But when they pay, they steal.

Life is a routine.

The work here is very hard,

from work to the bar,

trying to remember home.

I am going to visit

my beloved family.

I have a lot to tell you,

what life has provided me with.

Colleague's farewell.

I think I went very deep.

I tried to remember a little,

tried to find my real trip.

A YEARN LOVE

IN MY YOUTH,

I thought about Love

I grew up believing in it

with emotion from above.

Suddenly love arrived

without any explanation,

immediately was revived

causing a huge sensation.

My mind became blurred

with immense happiness

my body felt

she is so adorableness.

Love is so beautiful

when it touches our soul

is so plentiful

that within me calmness now holds.

I felt the love

from my other half.

It comes from above

now, together we laugh.

So it is wise that love is yearning

because when is shared

that love is earned

reason why we are paired.

She Loves Me

FROM THE DAY I SAW HER

I felt her palpitations

I went after her

And there was no communication.

I saw her again

in a festival

accompany her

he is now my rival.

But I insist

that she be convinced

when she saw me

what she missed.

On the third time

As I walk I saw her

She came to me

I embrace and kiss her.

And I asked her

why you elected him

without looking at me, she said,

I was never unfaithful to you.

TELL ME *my* LOVE

I AM INSPIRED

Loving you

I feel loved

Get close to me

You have accepted

The love that I gave you

You are to my liking

I am feeling you too

Tell me my darling

That you love me so

Tell me my heaven

That life comes with you

Tell me my love

That you would not go

Tell it to my heart

My heart is waiting for you

The time is now

And the love is so true

I am at your side

Feeling your happiness

Thanks sweetheart

There is no more loneliness

Thanks my darling

for making this come true.

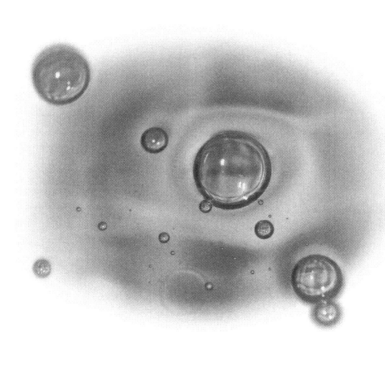

$\mathscr{L}$ooking *for* Love

IF YOU ARE LOOKING FOR LOVE,

you don't have to look very far,

I am here, here, here, here for you.

You will feel your heart beat,

at the tune so sweet

with the love that makes it complete.

You will never regret

if you say my love, yes,

because I will be there at your request.

So darling says sí, sí, sí

feel it and know what I mean.

you are the one born just for me.

If you are looking for love

you don't have to look very far

I am here, here, here, here for you.

You will feel your heart beat

at the tune so sweet

with the love that makes it complete

DREAMING with YOUR LOVE

—∽—

I WOULD LIKE TO SAY YOU DEAR,

I love you,

Once again to hear your voice would be

my heaven.

To taste your red lips and savor them

feeling your body as we grow so warm.

Toasting our love

I will wait for you.

Last night, I dreamed about our love,

you were close to me, my sweet,

in a colorful sundown.

It made it even more pleasurable.

I wish this was in real time,

breaking my solitude

with your honesty.

Share with me your happiness.

I want to tell you dear,

I love you.

Once again to hear your voice, my sweet.

133

to taste your red lips and savor them.

Feeling your body as we grow so warm

toasting our love

I will wait for you.

I Want You to Love Me

I WANT YOU TO LOVE ME

like I love you.

I don't want to hear a no

because I would die.

I want you to love me

without any condition,

Then you will feel my love

and a beautiful sensation.

I want you to love me

like I love you.

And the way I love you

I want you to love me and be true.

I want you to love me

like I love you.

And the way I love you

I want you to love me and be true.

I want you to love me

like I love you.

I want you to love me.

I am going to insist.

I want you to love me.

I feel a lot of emotion.

I want you to love me.

I am going to insist.

I want you to love me

I feel that grand emotion

I cannot live without you

Fulfill all my dreams.

IT'S NOT EASY to SAY I LOVE YOU

TO SAY I LOVE YOU, MY LOVE,

is not easy

there is fear to just pronounce it

because you don't want to be in the way.

To me, and maybe just me, my love

I fear to hear that it hurts

I don't want to suffer.

I prefer to stay quiet

and to continue to be in love.

with you, just with you, my love,

I want to be happy

and close to you,

living along with you,

with you in plenitude,

living it up with you

waiting for that illusion,

that one day you and I

will say to each other,

I love you with all my heart,

loving each other without being apart.

137

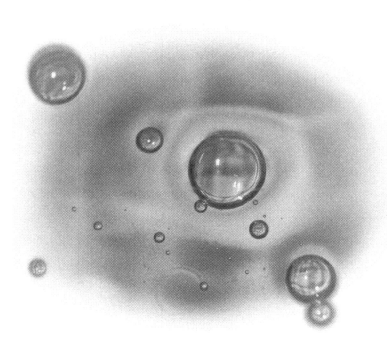

My Most Valuable was Lost

⌐

I HAVE CAUSED ME A WOUND
and it doesn't heal,
I left my family at the river
to intent to cross it,
believing that on the other side
being poor will be forgotten.

In my hometown we suffered
when I saw my children cry
because they ask me for food
that I could not provide.
They went to sleep hungry
wake up weak to go to work.

I left my beloved land
my parents and my friends,
to exchange them for coins.
The abuses from bandits
were constant, they would not allow me
to make ends meet, because I got rob.

139

To what do I owe this torment?

If I am not asking for things that are free,

I am looking for jobs that are honorable,

not to abuse or take jobs from any one.

But they continue to make jokes around

when I was trying to do an honest work.

Now that I have reasoned

I feel that I am alone

you can see hatred in my eyes

because others were just lazy

leaving behind unwanted pain

for being dishonest and greedy.

I hope I learned from this lesson

that the dollar is not everything in life.

My family is more important

instead of neglecting their lives.

Now, I am very frustrated

HAPPY TUNE

I AM TOASTING YOU MY FRIENDS
with this happy tune
and this great Mariachi
interpreting this special song.

The Mariachi makes us happy
I can feel it in my heart,
recalling the good times in México
as we prepare to sing our part.

Let's yell, our hearts, my friends
let it come with high emotion,
reviving all of us our soul
together with this special song.

Mariachi, Mariachi, Mariachi,
a symbol of a friendly nation,
with their traditional charro suit,
the pride of all its regions.

To sing songs from my town
dedicated to all ladies
our most beautiful human being
that all men admires.

Let's start the party
there's much to celebrate
and if you are happy
prepare yourself to sing.

Continue to have fun
let your feet feel the rhythm
as I say good-bye
with the Mariachi feel the freedom.

$\mathcal{I}$ Told You So

Precisely, I told you so,
that our love was meant to be,
you are the water of my life
and without you I get thirsty.

Your special touch is necessary
for a good and beautiful dawn,
I need that special feeling
because our love has just begun.

You are the light at high noon
that erases the shadow and darkness,
you give me much gladness
causing in me much happiness.

Your special touch is necessary
for a good and beautiful dawn,
I need that special feeling
because our love has just begun.

You are the light at high noon

that erases the shadow and darkness,

you give me much gladness

causing in me much happiness.

I hope that you have understood

that both of us have recognized,

and our souls has realized

the reason why we fell in love.

In Arizona a Mistake Was Made

I CROSSED THE BORDER; I AM NOT DOCUMENTED.

I left my family for need of money.

But also the hunger has forced me

to work for unmet salaries I was promised.

I didn't want to leave my land

or leave my beloved family.

The Coyote has taken advantage

by taking what little funds I've saved.

In Arizona I am hated by many

because I willing to do the work that pays low,

but from my salary they take sufficient funds

to fulfill social security and the income tax law.

I assure you that everyone has won with me.

The government, notary, and the lawyers,

since they hold their pants to tell the truth.

They used the vote as an excuse in the elections .

145

The Law 200 won and is now approved.

Citizens now work for the INS

and if I need to use any type of assistance

they use them as informants turning me in.

I want you to know that any benefits I used

is because in my case I already paid for them.

In my pay stub is well documented

but the traitors don't admit it, preferring to keep quiet.

BEAUTIFUL WOMAN

THE SUN HAS DISAPPEARED.

The moon is now out.

a brilliant star

like no other.

It is so precious,

that brilliant star

in the firmament:

that light she emits,

is equal to my lady.

For that love I die,

to love you deep within.

Make me yours,

my beautiful lady.

I become desperate

wanting your love.

I am faithful and therefore I will wait

Until that lovely woman arrive,

the one star I dream about,

desiring her has prolonged

my willingness,

following my wish

to love her with all my heart,

because she's all my happiness.

BEAUTIFUL SENTIMENT

I FEEL BUTTERFLIES WITHIN ME

Is your magnetism that I feel

This is the time that I presume

The only thing I know, that at last I found you.

I have a beautiful sentiment

Your warm of your body that I felt

Being close to you I feel content

Your essence is my complement.

What a marvelous thing

That at last I found you

And that I would not

Lose you anymore.

What a marvelous thing

That I will never leave you

I will always love you

For eternity.

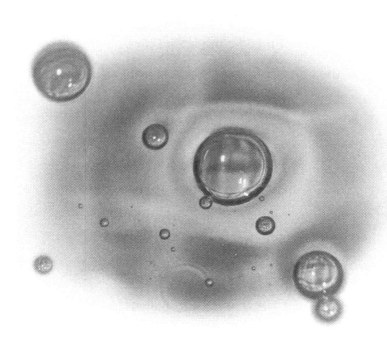

ℐNFATUATION ILLUSION

⌒

I CAN'T CONTINUE TO PRETEND ...ANYMORE

because I am in love, with you.

I no longer can resist

nor I can lie to you

not even a drink can prevent it.

Infatuation illusion

that betrays my heart

and spread it in my soul.

In an imperfect heart

no even that illusion

from the person that loves you.

I can't live without you

your friendship is infectious,

It is nice the way it feels

because I can share it with you

a lady that loves me.

Infatuation illusion

you see there is a reason,

My sentiment was well known

realizing my illusion

giving me ambition

now I am happy.

I can't live without you

your friendship is infectious,

It is nice the way it feels

because I can share it with you

a lady that loves me.

$\mathcal{I}$ Barely Met You

—

I've barely met you and I feel that we belong.

your personality attracted me to you

your eyes conveyed the message strongly,

and now, we are together feeling new.

Let it be, let it be, this love is for you and me.

Let happiness come, feel the calm of the sea.

Breath in the air so pure, so you will feel and see

that our destiny is for real; you just need to let it be.

They say that love is born at first sight,

so true because your inner self is so magnetic.

I can't wait to have you in my arms tonight

and make this so unforgettable and poetic.

As you can see the feeling was so true.

The first time we looked at each other,

created a special moment and I knew

that lovely night we spent together.

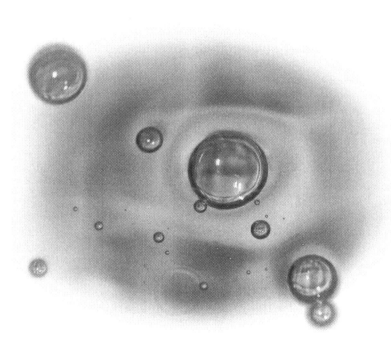

How Lucky Are *the* Ugly

SOCIETY DOESN'T HAVE THE PATIENCE
for those men who are ugly.
When they go to the dances
everybody makes fun of them.

But something is happening that is rare
that to their side they always have
the most beautiful babes
small, tall, thin, fit and fat.

Ugly, ugly men why are they so lucky
please don't take our only babes,
leave some for the handsome
don't be greedy and take them all.

Ugly, ugly men they are so greedy
they are abundant in every place,
they appear in every street
and you see them in discontents.

Now, all over the world

they are supported and respected

and the ugly gets even

with all the handsome men impacted.

Now, learn from this story

that all of us are ugly

What is worth here is the lesson

the inside is what is remembered.

EVERYBODY DANCE

EVERYBODY, THIS NIGHT
We are going to dance.
Take your better half
please don't pretend to beg.

The rhythm is contagious
Which began as playful.
Your body is so beautiful
It started to vibrate.

My eyes starting dancing
when you started to dance.
My feet started sliding.
I can't prevent the stance.

Moving our bodies
with much emotion,
don't let it forget
dancing this song.

Dance, dance

move your tiny waist.

Nobody, nobody

attempt to stay away.

Dance, dance

even with your mother-in-law

Nobody, nobody

Attempt to stay away.

COUNTRY IS in MY BLOOD

COUNTRY IS IN MY BLOOD

music in my soul,

all I need is love

to make my life whole, baby.

Won't you country dance with me, babe?

Country is in my blood.

Rodeo is my job

Don't be confused

and think that I don't care, baby.

It's you I love, babe.

It's you, you, I care about

you, you, I love the most

you, you, the one I want.

You're the one for me, I am the one for you

yes, our love is true.

Country is in blood

music in my soul

all I need is love

to make my life whole, baby

Won't you country dance with me, babe?

Country is in blood

Rodeo is my job

You don't think I care

and I understand you , baby,

but it's you I love, babe.

It's you, you, I care about

you, you, I love the most

you, you, the one I want

You're the one for me, I am the one for you

yes, our love is true.

You're the one for me, I am the one for you

yes, our love is true.

You're the one for me, I am the one for you

yes, our love is true.

$\mathcal{B}$AD NIGHT

YESTERDAY YOU WENT OUT FOR PLEASURE,

saying that it was with friends.

Today I learned

that you went to dance

so don't lie to me;

don't fake your love.

Everyone says of that night

that you danced all the time

with everybody who asked you,

and you went to spend the night

with the leader of the gang.

Why did you do that,

if I gave you all the love you wanted,

but you decided to choose your plot

and now everything wonderful giving is lost

I am leaving you

without saying good bye

so you can feel your lust.

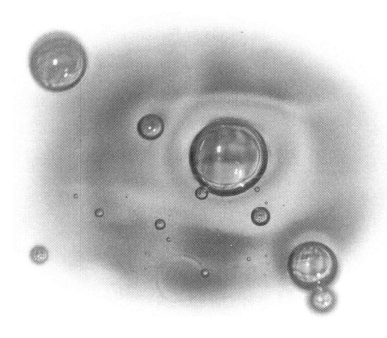

My Own People

IT IS SO BEAUTIFUL TO SEE PEOPLE UNITE

they will always have their mission in sight,

People willing to lend a hand,

to resolve any problem on demand.

But let's see the other side

discovering why we can destroy ourselves if we abide.

A person that don't take the time to mingle with his own

is the person that ignores the truth and pride.

Is the person that doesn't care about the education of the youth,

is the person that even if they don't want to accept it.

Puts tomorrow's generation in slavery neglecting its truth.

No, my friends this is not the road we want to take.

The ideal road is the one where we respect each other

like brothers because the other road is a disaster to take.

We finally notice the solution of this problem identified

so let's unite like coffee and cream combined.

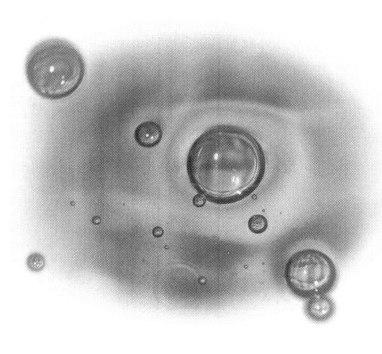

COMMUNITY SERVICE:
Volunteerism

IN ORDER TO OBTAIN A SENSE OF SELF WORTH
one must do worthy things with passion.
This is done by adopting a sense of community,
cleaning our neighborhoods and seeking solutions.

No act of kindness, no matter how small,
is ever wasted, yet much is achieved.
I learned early in life just follow your inner voice.
Receive an equal amount of fulfillment when you give.

Help leave the world better than when you arrived.
let us not be satisfied with just mouthing rhetoric.
Rhetoric is not enough; giving is the source of society.
spread the word, give everywhere you go, and make it historic.

Someday you may find your ideal job and would do it for less.
If you are lucky to find your calling, you may even do it for free for a
reason.
Join me and do community service and forever be blessed,
now you know that volunteering is my worthy passion.

165

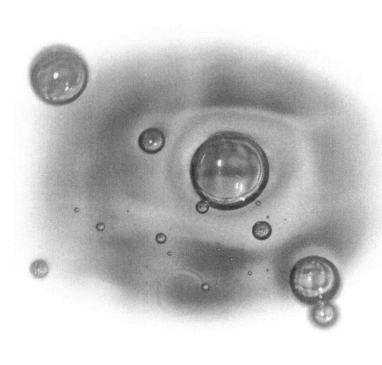

THE LIGHTING from AGUA PRIETA

~

ON THE BORDER, GENTLEMEN

a great horse race was held

Rafael Romero accepted

that his horse Relampago would race

with Chiltepin from Arizona,

Pinedo, horse owner, announced.

The American authorities

advised that both should run

in their own native land

each on their respective side of the fence,

Chiltepin in Arizona

and Relampago in Sonora.

In the year fifty-eight

Pinedo met with Romero

in the Copa Cabaña

to agree on detail.

Now that each horse

was denied to race on the other's turf

so grand horse race was born

167

with an International flavor.

Tickets started selling

throughout nearby towns

in two different countries

and bets were in the millions

as the shot signal sounded the start.

Both horses were even

they say it was so close

Without a doubt a good race.

Even though Chiltepin tried

the Relampago was the winner.

I toast with this song

to Leonardo Yánez, "El Nano,"

the composer of that famous song

the Moro de Cumpas, my brothers

Raúl Monreal salutes him,

and to Rafael Romero this is dedicated.

this is the end of the song,

hoping you like it,

of this international race,

while paying tribute to the past,

the Chiltepin of Arizona

and Relampago of Sonora.

TELL ME YES

YOU ARE THE LADY THAT I LIKE

that I like a bunch,

Just thinking of you

my heart gets excited.

From the day I saw you

I said you are for me,

Now I only ask

that you tell me the same.

Tell me yes, tell me yes

that you are in love with me,

Tell me yes, tell me yes

that you are in love with me.

I would do the same for you

I am saying yes to you, now

You are that lady

that I want just for me.

You are the lady that I like

that I like a bunch,

Just thinking of you

my heart gets excited.

From the day I saw you

I said you are for me,

Now I only ask

that you tell me the same.

Tell me yes, tell me yes

that you are in love with me,

Tell me yes, tell me yes

that you are in love with me.

I would do the same for you

I am saying yes to you, now

Your are that lady

that I want just for me.

THE BELL

As a bell, I was already designated

to arrive in Frank School in Guadalupe,

and to be in two pillars accompany

so when you pull the rope you will hear a sonorous sound.

Awakening the entire town to inform us

that the day started and time to adore us.

We as parents listened to the eco of the bell

that recollects our memories,

that idolizes our past in our history.

Send your children to Frank because they are my students

because from this school they will be the leaders of tomorrow.

and intelligent college students.

To all of us as parents to remember

the education of our yesterday.

It is noticeable that there is a movement of educators

that wants their children to learn to read

So as your formal alarm to awaken us

the bell offers you always that beloved signal.

THE CHEWING
GUM BOY

I AM THAT CHEWING GUM BOY
that found a hole in a fence
that opens the road
in a country with difference.

Now my knowledge got more broad
with vivid experience
and not giving up
to the unknown ambiance.

Creating bridges for those that follow
creating opportunities following leads
forgetting the pain and sorrow
allowing our gente to believe.

He became aware of his sacrifices
to those who want to succeed
to reach their objectives
allowing things to proceed.

For the new generations I care

I leave my finger prints for tomorrow

I want them to know that I dare

I will clean the road they must follow.

Obviously that is the goal

to open all doors

so that a children don't suffer

getting rid of remorse.

The opportunities will come

allowing minorities to succeed for the rest

that in one way or the other

getting an education is the best.

Provide work to those who endure

allowing success to the rest

for those who care

while our race reach their quest.

The First Kiss

THE FIRST KISS THAT WE SHARED

was recorded in our hearts.

I remember vividly what we said,

a devoted love that we impart.

The great time that we lived

we endear our hearts.

This is why we both feel

a love illusion in our charts.

In a short time we learned

the true meaning of our union

and my dream realized

through happiness comes communion.

We continue both to enjoy

the love that both cherished

that continues to grow

with the honest love we treasured.

THE FATSO

I MET A FATSO
with his girlfriend so thin
when they dance a slow song
everybody thinks it's so wrong.

Lots of people commented,
¿Is the fatso dancing alone?
or ¿Is his tie he has on?
No, no, no, is Paula and Paul.

With the food
I feel so happy,
seeing this diet
makes me want to eat now.

With food
I feel so happy,
seeing this diet
makes me want to eat now.

The fatso goes on a diet

his girl gains the weight.

The fat is now a bother

now he's aware that fat is there.

This story has an ending

the couple is just a dream,

commented Mr. Martin.

No, no, no, the fatso is Guillermo.

THE TOUR *has* COME

I AM A POET AND I INTEND TO BE

with sentiment to get to you.

The game to wait for us as minority

was just a dream.

But is time to cut this cord without end

and not even cheerfully,

to give to us the justice that we deserve

This is the only way this nation will be saved.

Treat me well, my friend, and I will do the same

treat me wrong and strong I will return.

I am not seeking power, simply looking to help you

so that you will learn my beautiful language and culture

The same way I learned to speak it and write it.

Help us with our development,

So that united we will make progress toward our common goal.

Our grandparents' land is now also yours,

for a simple error that even now you refuse to admit.

But what is done, is done.

So let us concentrate on the present and our honesty.

Let's behave like human beings the way God intended it,

to destroy the hell that no one wants.

The education that I have gained,

even though I had help from many from here and there,

will be put to good use,

to accept what belongs to us

without abusing it.

Allow me to develop

I will assure you that I will not boycott.

Understand that damage done has been forgotten.

But if you desire, it can be return, and it smells rotten.

To My Grandmother

TODAY I WANT TO PAY HOMAGE TO MY GRANDMOTHER, PAZ BARRÓN

That gave life to my mother and her sisters, with lovely reason.

Let's toast for her that now she watches us from heaven

From there she sends her protection and blessings without lament.

She sees us every day, wishing us to get together

And love each other in harmony

Continue each one of you with your obligations

That from here, our Lord and I will guide you without any conditions.

Now I want all you to give each other a hug.

It is the road that I have trace for you.

Celebrate my sons like if I would be right now with all of you

Because your friendship will break any wall of barriers.

WE BOTH CREATE a BONFIRE

THE DAY THAT WE SAW EACH OTHER
we created a bonfire
a kiss brought us both together,
creating an internal fire.

The coolness outside the room
was dressed the in pure white of snow
I was reassure that the love in fact was returned
that our relationship grew in turn.

Just now, I realized
when I felt her arms around me
following that inner feeling
my well being felt within me.

I prefer your freshness
and your exquisiteness
and I know my craziness
but I love you nevertheless.

This bonfire, this bonfire!

The night that we spent together

next to its warming fire

I realized we were lovers.

I assure you that I love you

that what I wanted is you

I no longer hold in my inner feelings

and my heaven is a true blue.

When I See You

When I see you

I desire you,

I want

that you be here

close to me

'cause I am your friend

and the motive

of our existence.

You recalled

that specific moment

that we loved each other

you to me and I to you.

It was so beautiful

our special care

being alone

close to you.

You see my darling

that is not a lie

In the contrary,

it is our real affair.

187

Because what's ours

I demonstrated

with such respect

and admiration.

Why Should It Be

I ONLY WANTED TO GIVE YOU MY LOYALTY

but you chose to leave me all alone

now, I understand everything

that maybe the first time I saw you

was wrongly misinterpreted

and now, I have to live with it.

I don't think that I need to drink to forget

this painful and deep sorrow.

But you are going to regret it and you will miss me

ungrateful woman,

with your venom

you will poison yourself.

Why should it be

that you just wanted to use me,

why should it be

that you wanted to deceive me.

If I gave you

everything I had

and I repent

because I don't even have you.

Why should it be

To wash my love this way,

why should it be

if I don't have everything.

because I don't have you

my heavenly dream my way

and now I noticed

that you were just a piece of dirt.

You Abandoned Me

YOU ABANDONED ME

and you didn't even let me know.

You just decided to leave

ignoring all our love.

But you chose the value of money

and I cannot calm this pain of mine.

You preferred to ignore our love,

Have thrown away our fine affair.

I ask God to forgive you

and not to abandon her happiness.

Play the song, "You Abandon Me,"

that singing soothes the soul.

I have to have more faith

so that I can feel the calm.

I don't want to suffer more

remembering the past.

Leaving behind the vanity

that in the future I will be loved.

You abandoned me

and you didn't even let me know.

You just decided to leave

ignoring all our love.

But you chose the value of money

and I cannot calm this pain of mine.

You preferred to ignore our love

have thrown away our fine affair.

I ask God to forgive you

and not to abandon her happiness.

Play the song, "You Abandon Me,"

that singing soothes the soul.

I have to have more faith

so that I can feel the calm.

I don't want to suffer more

remembering the past.

Leaving behind the vanity

that in the future I will be loved.

YOU INSPIRE ME

WHEN SHE SAW ME
she inspire me
and cause
an obsession.

When I saw her
she gave me
she gave me
an illusion.

Now I understand
what I feel
stupendous
emotion.

Even the rhythm
influence
and created
a sensation.

I thank you

my enjoyment

now I offer you

this melody.

There is happiness

what I have

to my friend

I owe it to her.

You Left Me

I HEAR THAT YOU LEFT ME.

That you negated

all of my love.

I hear that you forgot

that love you promised

to my heart.

Look, the wound

that you caused

became very painful.

I hope that she doesn't fall

even though she does not deserve

my heart,

but I will tell you

that I forgot you.

Now I am looking for another love

who will appreciate me

because I need to fill this vacuum

since you left me.

You hurt my heart

that false love,

not being truthful,

that violated me.

Consider my love

for one instant.

because she left me,

ignored me,

in an instant

left me alone.

BECAUSE I CROSSED

THEY SAY THAT I AM A WETBACK

They say I caused disorder

because I crossed territory

on the other side of the border.

They tell me I am a beggar

they tell me I am robber

because I do low paying jobs

that not everyone wants to cover.

But they have forgotten

when a family unites to eat

dinner at their table at home

I picked in the fields at the heat.

Lettuce, onions, tomatoes

cucumbers, peas and potatoes

enjoying a special house salad

as I sacrifice my back so valid.

They say that I am a wetback

They say I caused disorder

because I crossed territory

on the other side of the border.

They tell me I am a beggar

they tell me I am robber

because I do low paying jobs

that not everyone wants to cover.

$\mathcal{I}$ Love *my* Human Race

I WOULD LIKE TO TOAST

my human race

I don't intend to boast

even if it cost me to embrace.

It is the dignity

of my Indian blood,

Mexican and Spanish,

and I never give up.

I praise my human race.

I defend it constantly.

I don't lose a trace

I follow my path patiently.

There is nothing more beautiful

that my language and culture.

my land and the sky is plentiful

its essence rich and its water pure.

My God has chose

how I would be born.

What HE gave me

is worth everywhere.

So this is my human race.

Please don't you offend it.

In this society you see my face

we are in abundance, don't you forget it.

To Our Mothers

FIRST OF ALL I WANT TO TOAST AND PAY HOMAGE TO MY GRANDMOTHER

Dedicating this verses to tell you that you are not alone
Grandmother, you that continues to being a sovereign
that modeled an eminent to my mother and our sister
I offer you this words wrapped in fragrant carnations
so that you know how much you are value because we will always
be faithful.

Now follows my inseperable mother
on may 10th my life since birth I now more evident
Mother, mami, mama
o how I remember your arms, your caress and your face
Receive a kiss from your son that has always love you
You don't have any idea how much I value the fact you gave life.

A toast to my sister because she is also a model mother
thanking our grandmother and mother for their principles
She paid homage to both when she decided to be a mother
adding a child to the family and giving respect to both.
Receive both my thanks and gratitude for giving me the light of life

Your advices will be the gifts of life forever as I listen to your wisdom.

Last but also first is my lovely wife which is also a splendid mother

that always fills our home with lasting happiness and very affectionate

beautiful wife, loyal and graceful

Idolatrous and even sensible, like the petals of a rose

I want you to know dear wife on this special day

that you are the only one mother and we need you companionship.

All of you received our blessing

because you can be reassure that we will always honor you in

our hearts.

JOSEPHINA

EVERYBODY LET'S DANCE

with Josefina

making a lot noise.

To the tune of this song

with Josefina you will enjoy

dancing the cumbia now you belong.

Everybody let's dance

with Josefina

making a lot noise.

To the tune of this song

with Josefina you will enjoy

dancing the cumbia now you belong.

Everybody look how she dance, Josefina

when she makes her turn

with Juan, Don Juan.

Look at the baby

the men want to say

would you like to dance?

Everybody look how she dance, Josefina

when she makes her turn

with Juan, Don Juan.

Look at the baby

the men want to say

would you like to dance?

Everybody let's dance

with Josefina

making a lot noise.

To the tune of this song

with Josefina you will enjoy

dancing the cumbia now you belong.

Author Biography
An Exemplary Life

Raúl Sánchez Monreal, Jr. was borned in Nogales, Sonora México in the arms of very poor family but he was committed to change his destiny utilizing his strong will power. Even though his father left his mother when he was one year old and his youth lived was tough, he had to start working at a very young age assisting his mother who never gave up for her two children. But considering all the obstacles he had to overcome and his short youth time he had to face many challenges. He embraced each one of the challenges which reinforce the need to get an education because he knew that an education could bring a change in his personal life.

With no time to waist he went after his mission by taking one step at the time until he received his Bachelors Degree, Masters Degree and all course work completed to obtain his Doctors Degree. He immediately started recording his experiences and inspirations on paper utilizing traditional rhymes which created prose that his teachers began to notice encouraging him to continue. It was that moment that he began to refine his art and his passion for poetry taking it to a higher level penetrating people's hearts and emotions. Now, several of his poems are famous international songs that people sing and dance.

In the meantime Raúl's way of giving back to his community specially children was to assist in making a better world for all through promoting education, culture, human principles and family values allowing new leadership to surface that will make a difference in our society. He does this by example utilizing poetry to inspire as a tool to communicate with the human race.

www.RaulSMonrealJr.com

Testimonials

I f the towns have the governance that they deserve, perhaps also have the artist that they merit. Because a migrant town and marginated like a Latin in United States, they deserve an author like Raúl Sánchez Monreal, Jr. so that he can remind us about our roots and guide us to face with the seductive Anglo-Saxon culture. That's why the verses from Raúl are animated, encouraging, motivating…for "Get up once and for all!", get all your impulse so that you can overcome ignorance, exploitation and neglect.

Dr. Manuel Murrieta Saldívar

Founder and General Director of Editorial Orbis Press

www.orbispress.com

The poetry of Raúl S. Monreal, Jr. is a magnifying lenses by which the town can see themselves. Its simplicity reflects the sincerity of the author in permitting the most common readers to see themselves reflected in his verses in a profound simplicity. Monreal definitively touches the heart of the reader via the written word.

DAVID ALBERTO MUÑOZ, PH.D.

Author of books such Méxicalipsis; México: Identities Without Borders; The Other: Ramifications of Christianity

A UNIVERSAL THINKER whose inquietude to communicate in a simple melodic words that paint master pieces reflecting the sentiments of people. Raúl S. Monreal, Jr., a creative poet that captures the essence of a moment and then passes them in writing to archive those special unique times sharing them in this poetry book. Acquire it and you will experience and learn to value in "One Hundred Drops of Water" this treasure book of poems specially selected and collected by the author. I highly recommend this book of poetry for those who like to travel in time via a story telling format in a poetic form.

LORRAINE LUM CALBOW

Author

RAÚL S. MONREAL, JR. has lived a committed life. A life of community involvement, of civic leadership, of passion for the rich textures, colors, smells and sites that so many of us miss as we run ahead through each of our lives. Raúl is a multi-talented author, international songwriter and poet. Monreal's creativity provides warmth and insights in his most recent effort- One Hundred Drops of Water. Raul's poetry is open and honest. His poems can be enjoyed by the most ardent enthusiasts of poetry as well as by the common person who may be opening a book of poems for the very first time. Monreal's ability to fuse his deep personal insights into a wide range of life's little dramas, passions and realities breathes throughout One Hundred Drops of Water. Tenderness, love, life and all that he has experienced build the foundation for this wonderful book of poetry.

GREG PATTERSON

CEO/Owner, Andale Communication

www.andalecommunication.com

Printed in the USA
CPSIA information can be obtained
at www.ICGtesting.com
JSHW082202140824
68134JS00014B/390